THE WAITING PLACE

WHEN HOME IS LOST

AND A NEW ONE NOT YET FOUND

DINA NAYERI

PHOTOGRAPHS BY

ANNA BOSCH MIRALPEIX

CANDLEWICK PRESS

WHEN HOME IS LOST and a new one not yet found, children are sent to the Waiting Place.

Sometimes they go with their families . . .

and sometimes they are alone.

At first the Waiting Place welcomes you. It has heard of the wars, the famines and bombs in your home; it is very sorry. It has been waiting for you. It wants you to come in—and to stay.

INSIDE ITS GATED MOUTH is a dreary, lazy encampment where there is nothing to do but drift. Children wait, letting time slip away. They forget things: first their sums, street names, their best books. Then beloved faces, stories.

The Waiting Place doesn't mind. It wants more children and mothers and fathers. It doesn't want you to visit the nearby lake, to hike the frosted mountain, to learn your new language, or to work or build or learn. It craves your hours, weeks, years.

Here is a place that always sees you, it whispers in the night. *You must wait. Any day now. Tick tock. Why bother with plans? Sit, sleep, fight. Don't be caught unpausing.*

MATIN IS FIVE. He is from Afghanistan. His waiting place is a field of shipping crates turned into homes, just below a misty mountain where ordinary people picnic and hike. If a bird hits the metal crate at night, everyone jumps out of bed. The sound is like the angry men knocking, or debris smashing into the side of the small boat that carried Matin, his mother, and his sister Mobina to Greece— to Moria, the most evil of all the waiting places. "I don't remember it," he says, "because it was bad."

When left on his own, Matin only thinks of good things. He laughs all the time. When the Waiting Place tells him to nap or throw rocks or pinch his sister, he whispers back, "But Ahmad and Hashmat need me to find a ball. And they need a judge for the match. There's work to do." He sets his clock to help him remember all his responsibilities.

Matin doesn't have a father. But he once had a friend whose father worked at the airport. "When I grow up, I want to be the man who fills the planes with fuel. Without him, nobody can fly." Planes are freedom. One day, maybe Matin will fly in one.

He flies on his donated bike across the camp.

He makes a bow from an old bedspring. He defends against the older boys who have been at the Waiting Place for too long. "They want to make war," he warns his friends.

The older boys have hurt Matin in their wars. Now he pedals away fast. He has scars. He also has a rash on his tummy that won't go away. From the blankets.

One morning, Matin finds a ball in the trash. It's shaped like an oval; how strange. He jumps on his bike and pedals toward Ahmad and Hashmat. "I washed it and washed it and washed it," he says. "Look."

Sometimes Ahmad and Hashmat fight, as brothers do. For a long time after their last fight, Matin sat thinking, chin in hand, on the old bunk bed carcass outside their crate. When he had considered all the options, he told a story about how the warring older boys had become mean—it happened slowly, after many small battles. He negotiated peace between Ahmad and Hashmat and reminded them that good men watch out for each other, especially if they're brothers.

Every time an adult visits the Waiting Place, Matin greets them with one question.

"Auntie, Auntie," he asks a new lady. "Do you have papers? Who gave you papers?"

The new lady looks confused. "I'm Iranian," she says in Farsi. "For a long time when I was little, I lived in a waiting place, too."

"But now you have papers?" he asks. Papers mean you can leave the Waiting Place. Papers mean somebody has taken you in.

The lady nods. "America invited me to stay. I became American."

He says, "Those are good papers. You are very lucky."

MATIN'S OLDER SISTER runs into their crate and pulls off her watery blue school scarf. She rolls up a slice of lavash bread and settles in front of the tablet. She wants to watch the satisfying video, the one that brings the calm feeling. It shows how toothpaste can remove crud from an iron, how vinegar cleans a kettle, how baking soda whitens old sneakers. She also likes things fitting into slots, things being smoothed, things being colored in. Mobina is almost eleven and very good with the computer. She misses hers, left behind in Afghanistan.

In the Waiting Place, Mobina has two good friends. They spend all day together, reading, drawing, playing aunties. They defy the stupor and dare the Waiting Place to stop them. "We're true friends, not pretend ones like Shabnam and Setareh. Those two only think of themselves, I swear. They make so much drama!"

Shabnam and Setareh are always together. They met on the big ship from Moria, when
Shabnam walked over and said *Salam*. After that, they whispered secrets, giggled about
the other girls on the ship, and decided to be best friends. The Waiting Place gave their
families shipping-crate houses in the same row. Now they are neighbors! They live in B31
and B39 on the lower side of the camp.

Setareh means "star." Shabnam means "night dew." Their mothers think that their names suit them very well. Every day, Setareh wears a pink sweatshirt and a pink backpack and leads all the games. Setareh loves school. In Iran, she saved all her money for a metal pencil case. It was too heavy to carry in her backpack on the day they ran away.

Sometimes when Setareh is calling out teams, some of the girls forget to respond.

Since danger from home might follow them here, the Waiting Place has given some of the children *new* names.

They keep forgetting their new names.

All of Setareh and Shabnam's friends live in B camp, which is for newer arrivals. No one visits the A camp, the original camp, because the people there have lived in the Waiting Place for too long. Camp A is a ghostly place.

Nobody talks about it.

MONTHS AGO, as Setareh and Shabnam sat playing on a stoop, two new girls arrived.

New girl Kosar came from Iran, but she was Hazara, an Afghan ethnicity. Exactly like Setareh-Star! Hazaras are a minority group, and they're not very well treated by some Iranians.

New girl Shokrieh was Tajik from Afghanistan— like Shabnam-Night-Dew. In Afghanistan, Tajiks are one of the main ethnic groups. Tajiks don't know what it's like to be hated for your ethnicity—the color of your hair or the shape of your eyes—in your own home.

The Waiting Place, always stirring mischief, placed the newcomers, Kosar and Shokrieh, in the same shipping crate, right between old friends Shabnam and Setareh!

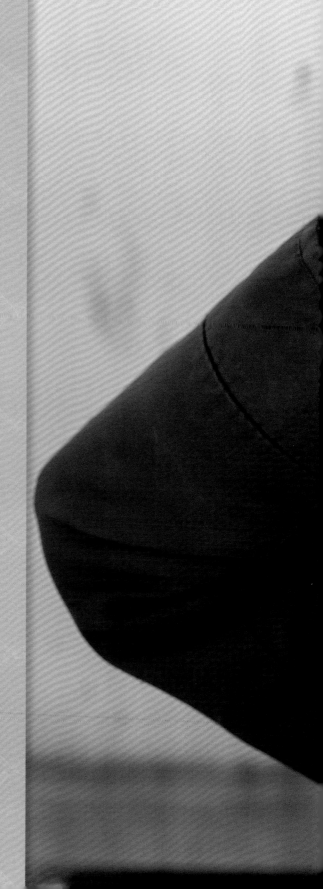

Kosar had a family of four. Shokrieh's family were six. They were good at sharing.

The families hung a gray utility blanket to divide the crate in half. They took turns cooking their food and ate on shared beds in their half of the crate.

Setareh liked new girl Kosar's feisty spirit. Shabnam had always been so quiet—just like night dew. Kosar was clever and creative. Sometimes, jumping on her bed, Kosar imagined herself taking off like a bird to another place. At home, she had been quick on the abacus and her teachers said she had a future in math. But she couldn't compete in tournaments in Iran because she was Afghan. Setareh was bookish, too. She started spending time with Kosar.

SATAR

"Setareh left me," said Shabnam to Shokrieh, her new friend, who was also quiet. Shokrieh knew many games with stones and could cartwheel clear across the camp.

"Did you come illegally?" Shabnam asked Shokrieh.

"How else?"

"I want to go to Canada," said Shabnam. "It's strong there. Strong countries protect travelers, like us. You should go to a strong country, too, okay?"

Shokrieh promised. After a moment, Shabham muttered again, "She left me."

Old friends Setareh and Shabnam didn't speak for a month. The Waiting Place whispered in their ear; it made them frazzled and nervous and sweaty with anger.

Setareh didn't have the words to explain: there are things you don't understand if your whole life you were a Tajik in Afghanistan. But being a Hazara, and in Iran? You *have* to be feisty and funny and in charge. You *have* to show you're a star. What other choice do you have? Kosar was the only other girl who knew what it was like to be the person who matters least.

Many days passed.

One day, Setareh wrote a letter for her first friend in the Waiting Place. She drew a heart on it. She hung it on her wall.

Salam. I am Setareh. I will go to school soon—after Christmas, of course, along with my friend Shabnam. Shabnam and I are the same age and we came together in the same ship. We played together and went up to the second floor of the ship twice. She is my best friend.

Now neither girl avoids B36. All the girls play there together. Once in a while, if someone donates meat, they eat Shokrieh's mother's delicious stew.

One day as Kosar and Shokrieh are playing, Shokrieh's big sister pierces her ears with a sewing needle. She tells Shokrieh to turn the string often so it won't stick. Shokrieh's older sister is cool. She has a lightning bolt in her hair. It's a scar from when their house was bombed, but she has a talent for fashion and she matches it with a lightning bolt shirt. Her scar is an accessory now! It's part of her brave new identity.

The Waiting Place doesn't like that one bit.

SOME DAYS, at 2 p.m., a bus comes to take the older children to school. The bus doesn't come every day. When it does, soldiers guard the gate while a Greek woman in a purple cardigan yells out words that sound *almost* like their names. Younger siblings watch as the older kids in their backpacks listen hard for their names.

On the way to school, Setareh leads the charge. Shokrieh and Shabnam don't mind. Sometimes Kosar gets annoyed. School makes it harder for the Waiting Place to cause fights.

Shokrieh's brothers Ahmad and Hashmat play outside, sometimes on the bunk bed carcass near their door. They like to collect feathers and explore. B36 is too full and, anyway, their older sister is cooking today.

Shabnam's brother Yusuf stays at home and dreams. Sometimes he has a nightmare: He is between a lion and a snake. He chases away the snake. He stands tall before the lion. It whimpers and flees. Yusuf is triumphant. But he can't fight the Waiting Place, because he can't see it whispering, moving, changing things. He gives in and waits and waits and waits, until the big sisters return from school at seven o'clock.

"Let's set our clocks," says Matin when he sees his friend Yusuf becoming listless and dreamy. He wants to make Yusuf wake up and fly! "Let's set our clocks and clear our schedules and meet the sisters at the bus, okay?" Yusuf nods at his friend, forgetting his nightmare.

As the sun goes down, the boys watch the big sisters appear near the gate. They all play together for an hour. Setareh shows them a trick: if you put raw pasta between your teeth, you can pretend to crack your neck. Just bite down on the pasta and *CRACK!* Her mother scolds her for wasting pasta—but then she sees the trick and laughs. At dusk, you can see the signs of joy all around—the flowery fence a father built, a deck, a pretty curtain—proof that the Waiting Place is losing.

Now and then, at sunset, when they're happy, the children wander into the original camp A. They pass by A31. Here live the girls who never come out. They are the trapped girls, nameless and faceless to everyone else. After so long in the Waiting Place, the sisters are vanishing.

NINA IS THIRTEEN. When she first arrived, she was eleven—just a kid. She's become a young woman here. Her name isn't really Nina. And her face can never appear in a photo. Her father watches over her everywhere she goes because the bad men from home have found out that her family is somewhere near the city of Ioannina. Every day, the men are getting closer.

Nina's little sister Minoo shares her small room. Their parents are afraid, and so Nina and Minoo are allowed no friends. They haven't been to school in two years. Nina spends all her time making things with her hands. In Iran, her father made buildings. Her mother made handicrafts. Here, Nina has plenty of time. She sits in her room and she makes things. Last month, she watched someone make an elaborate paper swan on YouTube. She made one of her own—it had a thousand pieces and took weeks, but it was flawless.

The Waiting Place can't keep Nina from growing tall and beautiful. It can't keep her from becoming a woman. One day two ladies visit, one with Spanish papers and one with American papers. "Can we take a picture with your masks on?" asks the lady with the Spanish papers.

"Not me," says Nina. "Baba says I have my adult face now. So even a mask isn't enough. Minoo's will change because she's young. You can take a picture of her."

There are teddy bears mounted to the wall. "People donate a lot of teddy bears," says Nina. "We don't need them. We put them on the wall."

Minoo poses barefoot for the camera. "Who does she think she is?" her father says, laughing. "A movie star?" Minoo had almost been lost, like cargo. The family had crossed the Aegean Sea in a beat-up old dinghy. When they climbed out of the little boat onto a big coast guard ship, Minoo refused to go with the officer. Instead she clung to her mother's back. They climbed so high, she thought she'd fall into the water. After that, she didn't speak for ninety days. Now she finally speaks, and her sister gives her anything she wants. Her parents too—she is their miracle girl.

"Do you have a boyfriend?" Nina asks the lady with the Spanish papers. "Is it normal in Europe for someone to date someone two years older?"

"Yes, it's normal," says the lady. "Do you have a boyfriend?"

"Yes," Nina says with a shy smile, "I have . . . someone . . . something."

Nina met a boy on her mother's secret Instagram account. He lives in Norway. She shows the lady photos of her class in Iran. "My teacher said I have a good brain," she says, using her new English words. "Maybe I can be a designer or a doctor." When the lady starts taking photos again, Nina is very careful. She covers the birthmark on her arm and removes a small photo of her sister's face from the corner of the wall.

The men can find you from a tiny photo—and they're getting closer. They want to steal the family and take them back to Iran. They appear in all of Nina's nightmares.

"Is Norway good?" she asks the lady with the Spanish papers.

"Yes, it is good."

"And America? Is America good?"

"I like it very much," says the lady.

"You've been to America?" Nina squeals. "That's so cool."

But now, the Waiting Place wants something else from Nina and Minoo. It craves more people. It wants to cram them all in. So it needs one of their rooms.

The Waiting Place has heard Kosar's family grumble. They share a room among ten people. It's impossible to live. The Waiting Place is afraid they'll run away. It offers Kosar's family their own crate. *Make yourself comfortable*, it whispers.

But that spare room has to come from somewhere. The Waiting Place eyes Nina and Minoo's room. It says they have to share with their parents now.

But Nina has a plan. She wants to go to Norway . . . and she knows now what the Waiting Place wants. The lady with the American papers told her. "To make someone wait is power. You can't give up that power. You have to work, to make things, to learn." The Waiting Place will be furious to hear this kind of talk.

THE WAITING PLACE wants children to stay. It wants them to forget the hours, the days. It doesn't want them to go to school, to see a doctor. It likes the dust to accumulate, the pretty paint to peel off the doors. It likes strange things: idle teddy bears on the wall, It whispers, *No need to bathe. You'll be gone soon anyway. What's another day?*

The Waiting Place wants you to be a child forever.

The Waiting Place never wants you to grow up.

AFTERWORD

by

DINA NAYERI

Refugee camps were nightmarish places even before 2020, when a new coronavirus sent many of us rushing into our homes and left the displaced alone and dangerously clustered, waiting for a new enemy to decimate them. In September 2020, the Moria Camp in Lesbos caught on fire. But Moria was hellish before the pandemic, before the fire.

Scenes of confused, exhausted children pushing through smoke are the inevitable outcome of the greatest collective failure of our time.

We create refugees and then we make them wait in bleak and hostile waiting places—a beastly limbo. We strip them, then abandon them for long stretches of time.

The average American and European citizen began paying attention to the problem of mass displacement around 2015—but it wasn't new. People have been displacing one another since we learned to walk across deserts and sail the seas.

I am a refugee. My mother is a refugee. Every war, famine, and flood spits out survivors. Every village that sits atop oil, or finds itself in the way of someone's ambition, sees its peaceful families robbed and cast out.

According to the United Nations High Commissioner for Refugees, as of 2020 the world contains an unprecedented 82.4 million forcibly displaced people. This number is so often used to frighten us—to make us believe that our trinkets and entitlements are in danger—that we fail to notice that nearly 48 million of these are *internally* displaced in their own countries. Another 26.6 million are refugees, and 4.9 million are asylum seekers. But even the smallest of those numbers, when used to drive fear, is disingenuous—because 73 percent of refugees live in countries neighboring their own.

Our leaders lie with metaphors, talking about floods and swarms into the West. Yet in 2019, fewer than 680,000 applied for asylum in the whole of the European Union. That is hardly a deluge. And the United States found a way to meet this weak trickle with all the disgrace and cowardice of a giant batting away a fly. The Trump administration created a refugee cap of 15,000—as if this is all that we owe to the world we have ravaged for resources. According to the 2020 census, that is just one human rescued for every 22,100 Americans.

After America's hasty 2021 exit from Afghanistan and the return of the Taliban, President Biden increased the refugee cap to 125,000. But the very notion of a cap still defies the Geneva Convention, which gives criteria for the suffering, not obligation limits for the privileged. Setting any number is especially appalling amid a humanitarian crisis that we have caused.

Our children will be ashamed of us.

We well-settled few use the oil or the land or the money from the war to make our lives more comfortable, more luxurious. And then when the victims come begging for refuge, we shut our doors, our eyes and ears. We ask, What if one of them is dangerous? What if they fill up our parks? What if they take our jobs, but also, what if they don't work at all and live off our taxes? What if their food smells too much like cumin? What if our children learn a strange tongue? What if our literature becomes too much like theirs? What if people cover their legs at the beach? What if blonde is no longer beautiful? What if my child marries a Muslim?

We see only ourselves—what we might lose, deviations from the landscape of now.

The 1951 Refugee Convention, a multinational treaty, sets a specific definition for "refugee" and requires all who meet that definition to be taken in. Setting a refugee cap is a blatant misinterpretation of that agreement. Refugees aren't ordinary migrants. How can you put a cap on need, on human duty?

Meanwhile, as authorities bicker and rewrite laws, refugees wait in camps.

Children wait, without school, without purpose, becoming idle.

No one talks about the waiting.

There are so many urgent needs: food, clothing, safety. We forget about the lost *time*, the lost purpose, dignity, ambition, and skill. But idleness is a curse. It robs children of their very identity and future.

In *A Lover's Discourse*, Roland Barthes writes, "*To make someone wait*: the constant prerogative of all power, 'age-old pastime of humanity.'" I felt this power exerted over me when I lived in a refugee camp. People love to keep each other waiting: as individuals, we do it to friends, to rivals, to colleagues, to lovers. And we do it as nations, too: to the most vulnerable, to show our power over them. We don't tell them how long the wait will be, though that would lessen the damage. Instead we choose to drive them mad.

As a mother, I feel the weight of this astonishing legacy as I teach my daughter about the world she inhabits. This is a house (*but not everyone has one*). This is a mother (*but some mothers are gone*). This is America, and England, and France (*at the door, there are men with guns, barring the way for some*).

It is hard to know what to say so that her luck doesn't make her blind. Raising a child who isn't astonished by the many accidents of birth would be my greatest failure.

We must change what we teach our children—because future generations are watching.

....

In 2018, I asked photographer Anna Bosch Miralpeix to accompany me to the Katsikas camp outside Ioannina, Greece. I chose Anna because her photos made familiar things seem eerie and new—with her lens, she brought out the darkness hidden in moments of celebration and the absurd in the most frightful scenes. I had visited this camp before. I knew some of the people. Anna and I rented a little house together near the camp. Each morning one of us made coffee and toast. We filled our pockets with candy for the children. Then we set off, me with my notebook, she with her camera and tripod.

Katsikas was full of refugees who had landed in the Moria camp on Lesbos island and who had been brought inland to live in this field of shipping crates. Because the most urgent dangers had passed, they succumbed to the darkness of the waiting. Some have been there for years, watching their children lose their magic and curiosity, watching them fall behind in school, grow lazy and bored, forget their hobbies and their sports. It is a tragedy to watch your children's potential slip away.

Anna and I craved to see these brave little people fighting back against the Waiting Place— the monster that wants to get inside you, to change you, to make you dull. I wanted to play with them, to enter their imagined worlds, to see the landscape inside their minds.

It was an education.

Every child was waging a private war against this monster, a true and tangible villain whose fetid breath made everything in the camp heavy and dreary and exhausting. But here is the part that gave me hope: many are winning! They are becoming braver, kinder, more astonishing versions of themselves. They are building their strong arms, their resilient minds, for when they finally rejoin our world. Maybe they can do this because childhood itself is a kind of waiting. It is full of pockets of boredom and fatigue, deep bouts of fantasy about the future. And in its way, the refugee camp makes everyone into children. There's something fertile about times of intense waiting (agonizing as they can be). In limbo, one can plunge into the imagination, create fantastical realms, perform creative feats.

I want luckier children to read about young refugees' battles with the Waiting Place. The Waiting Place is my Narnia, my Mordor. It is the land of Nod and of the Wild Things—a place of both dream and danger. I want these lucky readers to know that somewhere, their own future neighbors and friends are fighting this battle. When these friends finally arrive in America or England or France or Germany, they will be ragged and tired and sad. They will need strong arms to lean on for a while. And they will need friends to listen and to understand what it was like to confront the Waiting Place. Because one day, that monster may come for children whose feet have never left native soil. The monster wants us all—what adult has never felt the agony of being made to wait? We can't avoid it. But we can listen to stories of those who have been gripped in its clutches, learn what they know, and be ready.

GLOSSARY

Important Terms You Should Know

asylum: protection granted by a state to someone who is recognized as a refugee

asylum seeker: someone who has fled their country and is seeking international protection and refugee status. Their claim to be called a refugee (according to the legal definition) hasn't yet been accepted, and so they often live in refugee camps while they wait.

economic migrant: someone who moves to another country for economic opportunity or to escape poverty

European Union: an economic and political union of twenty-seven member states in Europe

(forcibly) displaced person: a refugee in the broader sense. A person forced to flee their home to escape war, persecution, danger, or disaster. Some displaced people do cross borders and become asylum seekers, recognized refugees, or undocumented migrants. But most displaced people are internally displaced.

internally displaced person: someone who is forcibly displaced by war or disaster, but has not crossed a border. Most of the world's displaced people are internally displaced, but often the larger "displaced persons" figures are erroneously or disingenuously used as a proxy for those seeking asylum.

Katsikas: one of Greece's many mainland camps, where refugees often go after they're released from Moria and other island camps

Lesbos: an island in Greece on which many refugees land

migrant/immigrant: an umbrella term for anyone who moves from their country to another. Because this term is often stigmatized (sometimes even lumped with "refugees"), wealthy people from Western countries have distanced themselves from it, using instead the word "expat" to describe their own migrations.

Moria: a camp on Lesbos where refugees are crammed together in terrible conditions, including overflowing sewage, shortages of food, inadequate housing for children, disease, and other dangers.

native-born person: someone who lives in the country in which they were born

1951 Refugee Convention: A treaty in which member states agreed on a policy of "non-refoulement," which means never sending refugees back into danger. The convention also set a definition for who is a refugee, and the member states affirmed their commitment to protecting the world's displaced people.

refugee: commonly understood to be a person who has fled their country to escape war, persecution, or other danger. However, the 1951 Refugee Convention specified persecution on the basis of race, religion, nationality, political opinion, or membership in a social group, a definition that's interpreted more and more narrowly by countries in order to reject refugees.

refugee camp: a place where refugees wait for asylum. Shelters in refugee camps might be tents, shipping crates, or other makeshift accommodations, or they might be converted buildings such as old hotels or residences. People living in a camp don't have a right to work and have inadequate access to health services and education.

refugee cap: the maximum number of refugees a country will take. Setting a cap is a violation of the spirit of the 1951 Refugee Convention, which sets clear guidelines for the treatment of refugees, whatever their number.

undocumented person: a person living in a country without permission, or someone who has been rejected for asylum. Many undocumented people are, in fact, refugees whose cases have been thrown out on technicalities or because of the narrowing interpretations of the 1951 Refugee Convention definition.

United Nations High Commissioner for Refugees: the United Nations Refugee Agency, established in 1950 in the aftermath of World War II and dedicated to helping the world's refugees

AUTHOR'S NOTE

Eventually, all that we do (and fail to do) is seen.

After reading this book to your child, think aloud together about what you might do to help displaced children. Can you assemble neighbors to vote? Can you send money and letters? Can you volunteer your time? One easy way to help is to send an old e-reader loaded with your favorite English books to a refugee camp. Don't send teddy bears. Send stories and words, weapons to fight the Waiting Place. Every book opens a door for an idle child. It nourishes creativity so that they can hang on to their private stores of magic.

I'd like to thank Anna Bosch Miralpeix for her incredible photography on this project. Thank you to the Columbia Institute for Ideas and Imagination and the charities Refugee Support and Second Tree. Most of all, thank you to the parents and children who shared their space with me and Anna, who played games with us and told us stories, who brewed us endless cups of tea, and who infused our visit to the Waiting Place (the setting of my own nightmares) with laughter, music, and childish wonder.

For my Elena. The Waiting Place wants children to stay children forever. And I confess

that sometimes I wish for that, too. But since you have to grow up, I hope you grow up in a world

where children aren't stuck behind closed borders, where you can go any place you like.

DN

To Inar and Berta. And to the children at Katsikas, and all the children forced to grow up too soon.

ABM

First paperback edition 2024

Library of Congress Catalog Card Number 2021946642
ISBN 978-1-5362-1362-1 (hardcover)
ISBN 978-1-5362-3311-7 (paperback)

24 25 26 27 28 29 CCP 10 9 8 7 6 5 4 3 2 1

Printed in Shenzhen, Guangdong, China

This book was typeset in Archer.

Candlewick Press
99 Dover Street
Somerville, Massachusetts 02144

www.candlewick.com